Presented to

From

Date

HERE IS

Christmas

by Donna Cooner art by Debra Reid Jenkins

WATERBROOK
PRESS

Here Is Christmas
Published by WaterBrook Press
5446 North Academy Boulevard, Suite 200
Colorado Springs, Colorado 80918
A division of Random House, Inc.

ISBN 1-57856-298-8

Printed in the United States of America
2000—First Edition

10 9 8 7 6 5 4 3 2 1

For Steven—who believes

—D.C.

For Carl and Evelyn Jenkins, with love

—D.R.J.

Here is the mother, tired and quiet,
whose heart is full of wonder.

Here is the husband, gentle and kind,
who smiles at the mother, tired and quiet,
whose heart is full of wonder.

Here are the animals, big and small,
who watch the husband, gentle and kind,
who smiles at the mother, tired and quiet,
whose heart is full of wonder.

Here is the stable, old and worn,
that shelters the animals, big and small,
who watch the husband, gentle and kind,
who smiles at the mother, tired and quiet,
whose heart is full of wonder.

Here is the star, bold and bright,
that shines on the stable, old and worn,
that shelters the animals, big and small,
who watch the husband, gentle and kind,
who smiles at the mother, tired and quiet,
whose heart is full of wonder.

Here are the shepherds, cold and afraid,
who run to the star, bold and bright,
that shines on the stable, old and worn,
that shelters the animals, big and small,
who watch the husband, gentle and kind,
who smiles at the mother, tired and quiet,
whose heart is full of wonder.

Here are the angels, glorious and gold,
who sing to the shepherds, cold and afraid,
who run to the star, bold and bright,
that shines on the stable, old and worn,
that shelters the animals, big and small,
who watch the husband, gentle and kind,
who smiles at the mother, tired and quiet,
whose heart is full of wonder.

Glory to God in the highest
and on earth—
peace—
goodwill toward men.

Thank you for the angels, glorious and gold.
Thank you for the shepherds, cold and afraid.
Thank you for the star, bold and bright.
Thank you for the stable, old and worn.

Thank you for the animals, big and small.
Thank you for the husband, gentle and kind.
Thank you for the mother, tired and quiet,
whose heart is full of wonder.

For here today, in the city of David,

a Savior is born...

He is Christ the Lord!